Original title:
The Meaning of Life, According to Wi-Fi

Copyright © 2025 Creative Arts Management OÜ
All rights reserved.

Author: Clara Whitfield
ISBN HARDBACK: 978-1-80566-024-8
ISBN PAPERBACK: 978-1-80566-319-5

The Interference of Insecurity

In a world where signals roam,
Connections spark like happy foam.
Yet I scroll and think what's true,
Is my password strong enough too?

I check my bars, they waver low,
My heart races, oh no, oh no!
Buffering dreams, they tease my soul,
While life's stream faces a troll.

Friend requests from all around,
But I fear their likes are just a sound.
Is my meme game up to par?
What if I'm just a blacked-out star?

So I reboot and change my name,
Hoping to escape this silly game.
Yet in this glitch of joy and strife,
I find my signal, much like life!

Fluctuations in the Heartbeat

Signals bounce and swirl about,
Loading joy, then doubt.
Packets full of hopes and dreams,
Glitches break those perfect themes.

Heartbeats sync with router light,
Connection strong, then out of sight.
Life's a dance of ups and downs,
Buffering smiles through silly frowns.

Navigating the Virtual Maze

In a web of endless scrolls,
Lost in clicks, we seek our roles.
Tangled wires and quirky memes,
Finding truth within the beams.

Redirecting every thought,
In this maze, we often rot.
Yet through chaos, laughter buzzes,
Surfing joy within our fuzzes.

Ciphers of Coexistence

Hidden codes that make us laugh,
Sharing moments in the graph.
A signal's wink, a router's sigh,
Friendship blooms through every byte.

Pings and dings, our hearts align,
Uploading love, a constant vine.
Through all the latency we face,
Connection's warmth, our saving grace.

Embracing the Invisible Network

Waves unseen, yet felt so clear,
We connect despite our fear.
In every hiccup, every lag,
Together, we can never drag.

A Wi-Fi hug, a digital squeeze,
Laughter echoes, hearts at ease.
Embracing voids, we find our way,
In this mesh, we choose to stay.

Frequency of Longing

In a world with no bars,
We search for a spark,
Connection fades away,
Like a shot in the dark.

Our hearts lose the beat,
When the signal's too weak,
We long for the touch,
But our Wi-Fi is bleak.

Scrolling through memes,
In a lonely abyss,
The router's our guide,
In digital bliss.

So we tether our hopes,
To the cloud in the sky,
For love's just a login,
That we seldom can try.

Echoes in the Signal

In the bandwidth of life,
We echo our dreams,
Buffering moments,
Are not what they seem.

With every dropped call,
And with every missed ping,
We laugh at our fate,
And the joy that it brings.

Like a ghost on the net,
With a lag and a glitch,
We navigate love,
With a click and a switch.

So we dance through the haze,
In the fiber and light,
For our hearts are still there,
In the dead of the night.

Searching for Data in the Void

Lost in the ether,
Where no signal resides,
We seek out connection,
With the moon as our guide.

Our hearts take a dive,
In a sea of dismay,
Just a whisper away,
From a magical stay.

Buffering feelings,
Like a stream that won't load,
We laugh through the woes,
Of this funny old road.

In the dark we will find,
A connection so bright,
To the void we will send,
Our quirky delight.

Interfaces of Infinity

Where the packets do dance,
In the circuits of time,
We chase after love,
Like a rogue little rhyme.

Emojis in bytes,
With a wink and a grin,
Each ping brings us closer,
To where we begin.

In the mesh of our hearts,
We load and we share,
Together we roam,
In this vast, vibrant air.

So let's surf through the dreams,
And enjoy every wave,
For a network of laughs,
Is the bond that we crave.

Unplugged Insights

In a world where signals fly,
Every drop makes the routers cry.
Connection lost, oh what a plight,
Without the net, we're out of sight.

Boot up again, see who's awake,
Scrolling memes for goodness' sake.
Life's a stream, don't join the fray,
Just find the password, and hit play.

Bytes of Belonging

In the land of endless pings,
We find joy in little things.
Sharing laughs through fiber lines,
Uploading love amidst the pines.

Check your status, wave hello,
In this space, we steal the show.
Bits and bytes, our hearts entwine,
Finding warmth in the online.

Resonance Between the Routers

Wi-Fi waves dance through the air,
Connecting souls with little care.
A browser tab, a friend request,
Proving we're at our social best.

Router whispers, 'Can you hear?'
In this zone, we have no fear.
Bonding over memes so bright,
Chasing pixels into the night.

Virtual Reflections

Gazing at screens, we laugh so loud,
Behind our devices, a vibrant crowd.
From buffering woes to viral glee,
In every byte, we find our spree.

Chatting in emojis, so much to say,
In this network, we find our way.
Life's a scroll, so let it roll,
Together we make Wi-Fi whole.

The Light of Connectivity

In the glow of signals bright,
We find our paths, our joys, our plight.
A buffering heart, a pixel smile,
Connecting people, mile by mile.

Through routers' hum and endless scrolls,
We tap away, revealing souls.
A meme, a gif, a viral laugh,
In this vast web, we share our craft.

Transcending Through Transmissions

Dancing bytes in cosmic waves,
Spinning tales of brave new slaves.
Notifications sing and cheer,
As life unfolds right here, right here.

A glitch, a lag, a sudden freeze,
Yet still we search for subtle keys.
To unlock doors of brand-new streams,
And stream our wildest dreams, it seems.

Connection in Invisible Frequencies

Lurking close, yet far away,
Waves of laughter find their way.
Invisible links, a sneaky dance,
In the digital void, we take our chance.

Between the bytes, in scattered noise,
We bring together all our joys.
A cat video, a long-lost tune,
Life's a meme, under the moon.

Signals Between Souls

Hey, are you online? A message bright,
Sparks of friendship in the night.
In every ping, a heart that swoons,
We share our secrets, hidden tunes.

Through email chains and video calls,
We break down walls, we share our falls.
A network strong, we rise and dive,
In this wired life, we truly thrive.

Wavelengths of Wonder

In a world of ones and zeroes, we roam,
Searching for signals to feel at home.
Packets of joy, laughter's delight,
Connecting our hearts, day and night.

Buffering dreams on a digital stream,
Wi-Fi's our guide in a whimsical dream.
Signals may waver, but always persist,
Life's silly moments can't be missed!

Bridging the Gaps

Roll out the routers, let's link our souls,
In bandwidth of friendship, we reach our goals.
Interference laughs, we dance through the net,
A signal of humor, you won't soon forget.

Cables may tangle, but hearts stay clear,
Sending good vibes with every cheer.
That patchy connection might bring a frown,
Life's a big download, so let's not drown!

The Unwritten Network

Unplugged from chaos, we sit and share,
In the web of laughter, there's love everywhere.
Roaming through moments, no limits in sight,
Capturing joy like a viral highlight.

No terms of service limit our cheer,
In the cloud of friendship, you're always near.
Wi-Fi may flicker, but the fun won't cease,
With every connection, we find our peace!

Life's Signal Strength

Find the hotspot where spirits ignite,
Together we're stronger, our future is bright.
Emojis sparking, the laughter it sends,
Chasing connection with family and friends.

Download a smile, upload some cheer,
Sharing our stories, it's crystal clear.
In this crazy network, we all play a part,
Wi-Fi may fade, but love's off the chart!

The Invisible Thread

In the ether where signals flow,
Invisible threads help us grow.
With passwords tight and routers near,
We laugh online, spread good cheer.

Yet lost in lag, we sit and stare,
As buffering hides our witty flair.
Connection drops, a quiet sigh,
In pixels clear, we still comply.

Circuits of Connection

Through circuits vast, we send our love,
Like tweets and memes fit like a glove.
Wi-Fi whispers, 'Come out and play!'
As digital friends light up the day.

But when the modem starts to hum,
We ponder deep on what's to come.
A world so bright, yet plugged away,
Can happiness be a game we play?

Distant Signals

From distant lands, our voices blend,
Each chime a chance to make a friend.
In cyberspace, we roam so free,
A quirky bunch, just you and me.

Yet signals fade, the screen goes black,
A world of memes now slips the track.
We fumble through the Wi-Fi waves,
Is this the joy that tech enslaves?

Life's IP Address

An IP address, a quirky sign,
A number line that's quite divine.
From bytes to bits, we try to know,
Is laughter found in status show?

Yet when the router goes on strike,
We wonder if we've lost our hike.
Wi-Fi wisdom in every byte,
In this strange dance, we find our light.

The Frequency of Freedom

In a world of signals bright and clear,
We roam through ether with naught to fear.
Connecting dreams in a wireless spree,
Chasing the bandwidth, oh so carefree!

Lost in the range, clicking 'refresh',
Living for pings, we are truly blessed.
Though life may buffer, don't you despair,
Just a few bars and we've got good air!

Language of the Links

In the web of data, we find our chat,
With a meme on the side, and a cat pic sat.
Searching for love in the streams of code,
Love bytes and emojis, our simple ode.

Passwords and firewalls safeguard our souls,
Like digital knights, we defend our goals.
Yet if you forget one, oh dear, what glee—
It's like losing your shoes at a dance, you see!

Tethered to Tomorrow

In cafes we huddle, connections alive,
With Wi-Fi so strong, our spirits thrive.
But drop that signal, and oh what a mess,
We feel disconnected, like teens in distress!

Yet every lost signal shows us a way,
To cherish the moments, come what may.
So tether your heart to each fleeting chance,
And dance in the chaos, oh what a dance!

The Power of Presence

Sometimes we log in, only to scroll,
Missing the moments that fill up our soul.
With devices in hand, we laugh and we cheer,
Yet face-to-face chats can bring us more cheer!

Disconnect to connect, a twist in the plot,
Real life is the Wi-Fi that chaos forgot.
So power off, friends, let's share a laugh,
In the joys of real life, let's find our path!

Frequency of the Heart

In the realm of clicks and pings,
Love's a hotspot, no strings.
Buffering when you're alone,
But share a meme, and you're home.

Data plans can't hold us back,
When hearts sync on the same track.
Forget the movies, leave the snacks,
We're just out here sharing laughs.

Wi-Fi waves bring friends so near,
Connection's strong, there's nothing to fear.
With every password, trust is born,
Through signal strength, we are reborn.

Navigate through life's wild surf,
Find a laugh for what it's worth.
In every byte and every tag,
End of the day, we'll just brag.

Surfer of the Signal

Riding waves of bits and bytes,
Hanging ten on weekend nights.
Surf that bandwidth, catch that stream,
Living life, it's quite the dream.

No need to fight to find your flow,
With every login, friendships grow.
Laugh at lag, it's just a game,
In this connection, we're the same.

Route your heart to every friend,
In this wild web, we'll surely blend.
High-speed love, no need to chase,
Just hold on tight, embrace the space.

Pixelate the highs and lows,
Through tangled cords, the laughter flows.
Every giggle, a footnote bright,
In this café of Wi-Fi light.

Pulse of the Connected

Tap into joy, it's quite the rush,
Every heartbeat feels the rush.
No need for maps or GPS,
Emojis help us find success.

Through the routers, we exchange,
In this matrix, nothing's strange.
Send a meme, it brightens days,
In digital worlds, we find our ways.

Pulse in sync with each liking touch,
Friend requests mean so very much.
Scroll through life with humor's bend,
In this life of Wi-Fi, we extend.

Fingers dance upon the screen,
Our bonds stronger than they seem.
Connected with a single click,
Life's a network, share it quick!

Streaming Our Stories

Once upon a download's tale,
Of cat videos that never fail.
A flicker here, a meme with flair,
We stream our worlds with loving care.

Click and play, don't miss the beat,
Life's a playlist, feel the heat.
In every bitrate, joy resides,
In chatrooms, our essence glides.

Sync your heart, don't hit rewind,
In this forum, friendship's blind.
We share our dreams; we share our woes,
Across this network, laughter flows.

So here we stand, both near and far,
Guided by our glowing stars.
In Wi-Fi waves, we shout and cheer,
Together we laugh, with love sincere!

Love in the Bandwidth

In a world so wired, connections arise,
Our hearts in the cloud, as bright as the skies.
Pixels and pixels, we flirt on the screen,
Love's lost in packets, yet still feels serene.

Emoji hearts sent, we giggle with glee,
But buffering moments, they frustrate me.
We dance through the bandwidth, both close and apart,
Yet your Wi-Fi syncs beautifully with my heart.

Fading Signals

Oh signal so strong, how you wane and you fade,
Just when I need you, you play a charade.
My heart skips a beat when you're full of surprise,
But one little glitch makes me roll my eyes.

I search for your presence, I pan with my phone,
Anxiety rises, I feel all alone.
But wait! There you are, just a bar on the right,
In fading signals, I find my delight.

The Cache of Existence

I stumbled upon something stashed in a byte,
A cache of my memories, stored in the night.
Scrolling through laughter, through joy and despair,
Each click is a treasure, a digital air.

Wi-Fi can't hold every memory I hold,
Yet each little moment, a story retold.
In browsing the past, I chuckle and sigh,
For every lost link, I learn how to fly.

Flux and Flow

Life's a stream of data, constantly flows,
With pings and with pongs, as the bandwidth grows.
We dance in the ethers, in ones and in zeros,
Tripping on laughter, we're all comic heroes.

Connection may falter, but joy's here to stay,
Just reboot your heart, let your worries sway.
In waves of tomorrow, let's ride the high tide,
In flux and in flow, love is our guide.

Navigating the Digital Landscape

In a world where signals dance,
We find ourselves in a trance.
Loading dreams with every click,
Wifi waves, a magic trick.

Router spins like a DJ,
Turns our chaos into play.
Buffering thoughts, we try to type,
Missing memes, we laugh, we gripe.

Packets flying, hearts aglow,
Lost connections steal the show.
Just like life, we roam and seek,
A little lag, we're still unique.

So here's to screens and endless scrolls,
In cyberspace, we find our roles.
With every ping, a chuckle shared,
In this vast net, we all are paired.

A Symphony of Connections

Frequencies play a lively tune,
In the twilight, finding our boon.
Data flows like a river grand,
Bringing souls hand in hand.

Clicking hearts in a chatroom bright,
Typing fast into the night.
Echoes of laughter through the wires,
Connectivity lifts our desires.

Emoji faces, a virtual grin,
Like a dance, we spin and spin.
Every refresh, hope's new chance,
An online world, a joyful dance.

So let us toast to the great web spun,
Where distance fades, and joy is won.
With a giggle and a joyful cheer,
In this realm, we hold each dear.

Glitches and Grace

Sometimes life just doesn't load,
We trip and stumble on this road.
Glitches come, but oh so funny,
Turning frowns to smiles, sweet honey.

A disconnect can bring delight,
Pixelated hearts feel so right.
Wi-Fi hiccups, a charming spree,
Glitches bring friends, you and me.

Reboot the joy, and let's restart,
Each lost signal a work of art.
In the chaos, a grand design,
We find the laughs, tangled in the vine.

So raise a glass to every blip,
To life's quick twists and every slip.
Here's to connections, strong and true,
Where every glitch leads back to you.

Pixels of Perception

In a pixelated world we roam,
Through screens, we build our funny home.
Each meme a snapshot, a precious find,
In digital realms, we unwind.

Wi-Fi waves like a playful breeze,
Tickling our brains with such ease.
Data bursts, ideas collide,
In vibrant pixels, we take pride.

Fuzzy lines may blur our view,
Yet humor shines, bright and true.
Connect the dots, let's laugh and cheer,
In this pixel party, bring good cheer.

So let us groove in this networked space,
Finding joy in every place.
Through digital chaos, we'll persevere,
With pixels of laughter, sincere and clear.

Surfing the Life Line

Fingers dance on buttons bright,
Chasing signals in the night.
Life's a wave, we surf and glide,
On a router's joyful ride.

Friends in pixels, laughter flows,
In a world where meme time grows.
Caffeine fuels our midnight clicks,
In this realm of playful tricks.

A Canvas of Connectivity

Pixels paint our daily tales,
In this web, there's no one fails.
Upload dreams and download fears,
Connections last for endless years.

Wi-Fi signals, love's embrace,
Streaming fun at a frantic pace.
We share our snacks and meme delights,
In the glow of screen-lit nights.

Driftwood in Data

Lost in data, float we must,
Like driftwood, we find our trust.
Stream of thoughts, a joke or pun,
Life's a gig, we laugh and run.

With a signal strong and true,
Every glitch feels like déjà vu.
Off we drift, no need for oars,
Just a click, then we explore.

Unplugged Reflections

In a world where we forget,
Wi-Fi's warmth is the best bet.
Unplugged life feels quite absurd,
But then again, have you heard?

Roaming free without a care,
Signal lost, just nature's air.
We laugh at how we're oft ensnared,
In a life of likes, unprepared!

Unraveling the Code

In the realm of bits and bytes,
A dance of signals ignites.
We search and scroll with glee,
As routers whisper secrets to me.

A flicker here, a glitch there,
Life's password rings in the air.
Connect the dots, don't be shy,
What's the meaning? Oh, just Wi-Fi.

The Protocol of Being

To connect or not connect, that's the quest,
Packets of joy put to the test.
In this chat room of existence,
A laggy life lacks persistence.

IPs and dreams collide,
A network of souls, far and wide.
Ping me a sign, a little delight,
As we surf through day and night.

Surging through Silence

In the silence of a dropped call,
Life buffers, but we still stand tall.
Downloading laughs, uploading tears,
Skip the ads of all our fears.

A signal lost, then found anew,
We roam the cyberspace crew.
With every bar that dances bright,
We giggle through the endless night.

Bandwidth and Belonging

Life's bandwidth stretches wide,
In this virtual joyride.
With each reset, a chance to see,
Our connection's wild esprit.

So here's to the pixels and memes,
To life, laughter, and the dreams.
Load up on smiles, let's all chime,
In this network, we'll dance through time.

Transcendence in Tech

In a world of screens that glow,
We seek connections high and low.
Loading dreams on fiber threads,
Chasing bytes, no time for beds.

With every ping, my soul ascends,
Through data streams, I find new friends.
A buffering beach, it calls my name,
In the cloud, I'm never the same.

Router prayers sent to the sky,
Hoping for bandwidth as I try.
My inner self on the latest app,
The universe in a Wi-Fi gap.

In every quirk, my spirit's found,
Amongst the signals all around.
With memes of wisdom in my feed,
My quest for truth is well-compleased.

Silent Signals

In silence, signals bounce and play,
Invisible waves guide my way.
A 'no service' zone, my heart does pout,
As I shout to the void, 'What's this about?'

Oh, digital friend, where art thou gone?
Searching for you from dusk till dawn.
Yet here I am, a Wi-Fi sage,
A router warm, a fabled page.

My inner thoughts streamed bit by bit,
Translating feelings, never quit.
The emoji laughs bring forth a cheer,
In binary code, love draws near.

Byte-sized giggles ignite my mind,
In hidden networks, truth I find.
A LOL echoing through the dark,
In silent signals, I leave my mark.

Harmony in the Hotspring

A hotspring bubbling, warm delight,
Wi-Fi waves flow like pure sunlight.
In steam and laughter, we connect,
All devices here, perfect specs.

With every splash, a text appears,
Sharing giggles, banishing fears.
Hot tub therapy, digital bliss,
In a world of signals, I find my kiss.

Fish lip-sync to the latest trend,
While I refresh, my soul to mend.
In wireless warmth, I soak and smile,
Connected here, across each mile.

Life's a meme drifting like heat,
In pixel hangs, our joys repeat.
The hotspring hums a cosmic tune,
With laughter blending in the afternoon.

The Cosmic Connection

Under the stars, I search for light,
Wi-Fi dreams take off in flight.
A cosmic dance of dots and dashes,
In zeroes and ones, my spirit crashes.

Each packet sent like a wish to roam,
Finding my place, the universe home.
Galaxies ping as I hit refresh,
In this vast web, I find my flesh.

Life's a router, spinning fast,
With memories saved, a network vast.
As I upload my thoughts and fears,
The stars reply, "Don't disappear."

So here's to signals that travel wide,
In cosmic realms where dreams abide.
Laughing at life, with Wi-Fi pride,
Together in this cosmic ride.

Waves of Existence

In the air, signals ping and play,
What is life? Just parts of the array.
Connecting dots like a cosmic net,
Yet my phone still says, 'No internet!'

Data flows like a river wide,
Streamed moments we laugh and abide.
Buffering dreams, we click and scroll,
Searching for meaning, or just a new role.

Life's a hotspot, we tap and browse,
Finding joy in a cat video mouse.
Downloading wisdom, a meme or two,
Eternal questions posed by a blue hue.

Here's to passwords, we joke and stew,
Living large in the digital zoo.
Like Wi-Fi waves, we go up and down,
Chasing connection all around town.

The Network of Unsung Dreams

In tangled wires our thoughts reside,
Through signal strength, we must confide.
Dreams uploaded, hopes on high,
Yet sometimes they freeze, oh my, oh my!

We roam the net like daring fools,
Finding life lessons in TikTok schools.
Remember, kids, it's just a game,
Not every ping is fortune or fame.

Lost passwords are a pesky plight,
Like finding meaning in a sneeze at night.
Still, we laugh as we scan the screen,
For every glitch, there's joy unforeseen.

Unplug the chaos, let's go outside,
Chase the sunlight, let's not abide.
But we'll be back to check our feeds,
For memes and dreams, our daily needs.

Bytes of Purpose

Small packets of fun ride the air,
Life's a download, a cheerful affair.
Each byte contains a sliver of cheer,
Just like the Wi-Fi we hold so dear.

Buffering laughter, we click and pause,
Searching for answers, we give applause.
Living through updates, with zeal we share,
Hunting for purpose without a care!

Enable the hotspot, let the joy flow,
Savor connections we yearn to know.
While roaming the web, we analyze,
Finding deep truth in the silliest lies.

So surf the waves, find your delight,
This digital journey feels just so right!
With every signal, we gather and gleam,
In bytes of purpose, we stoke the dream.

Unseen Links

Invisible bonds in a world so vast,
Connections forged, no need to ask.
Life spins on as we swipe and scroll,
Invisible threads weave heart and soul.

We giggle at memes that spark a light,
Finding each other in the dark of night.
Behind each screen, a laugh, a cheer,
We share the moments that bring us near.

Unseen links that never break,
In every friend request, a new mistake.
Like a missed text or a dropped call,
Life's all about the rise and the fall.

A signal weakens, yet we still try,
To connect the dots and reach for the sky.
In funny moments, we'll always find,
The joys of existence, to which we're blind.

Echoes in the Ether

In the realm of signals, we all reside,
Chasing bars and dots, it's a fun-filled ride.
Packet loss and lag, make us laugh and sigh,
Yet we all keep scrolling, as bits zip by.

Wi-Fi whispers secrets, with every connection,
Our lives in the cloud, a digital affection.
Buffering dreams, in pixels we trust,
Finding joy in glitches, it's a must!

Data Streams and Destiny

In the stream of data, we find our role,
Sending memes and gifs that brighten the soul.
With every refresh, laughter's on the line,
Swipe right for joy, it's a sign!

Bytes of laughter stitched in the air,
Connecting souls, with whimsical flair.
But oh, the irony when it fails to load,
Life's a Wi-Fi joke, on a merry-go-round road!

Life in a Hotspot

Clouds overhead, but I'm tethered here,
In a world where the Wi-Fi is my only cheer.
Despite poor reception, I'm feeling so grand,
Searching for that signal, hand in hand.

Hotspot hustle, it's a quirky dance,
Ping me, baby, give connection a chance.
We'll stream our dreams, on this digital bliss,
Downloading laughter, a delightful twist!

Transmitting Intentions

With every click, our hopes take flight,
In the vastness of cyberspace, we find delight.
Friend requests like butterflies in bloom,
In this Wi-Fi garden, there's always room.

Transmitting wishes on a cosmic wave,
As bits and bytes turn, learn to behave.
Mash those buttons, and let joy unfurl,
In the network of laughter, let's give it a twirl!

Wi-Fi Whispers and Life Lessons

In cafes and in homes we sit,
Our lives streamed on a tiny bit.
Reconnect when feeling low,
A signal strong and heart aglow.

Buffering moments lead to glee,
Life's quirks load so effortlessly.
A shout-out here, a meme there too,
Wi-Fi knows just what to do.

Drop the call, don't lose your thread,
Funny quirks fill hearts instead.
Life's best bytes come through with ease,
In laughter's warmth, we find our peace.

So pause, refresh, and take a sip,
It's all a fun, chaotic trip.
In the mesh of signals we learn,
To live and love, and wait our turn.

The Unseen Threads of Connection

Invisible waves connect us tight,
Through routers, beams, and laughter bright.
Friendships load with just one click,
A dance of pixels, oh so slick.

Sometimes the signal drops, oh dear,
But don't you fret, just hold it near.
Buffering hearts keep us amused,
With every glitch, we're still infused.

Data packets of joy we share,
In the web of life, we all declare.
Send a meme, or a funny pic,
In every file, we find our trick.

The world may seem to slow and freeze,
But laughter's what brings us to our knees.
Reconnect, refresh, and have some fun,
In this wild network, we are one.

Pixels of Purpose

Pixels dancing on our screens,
Life's just funny little scenes.
Wi-Fi waves and joyful flows,
Send us where the laughter goes.

From the couch to the café booth,
We share our lives—what's the truth?
Load your heart with memes and cheer,
The best connections happen here.

Every glitch becomes a jest,
A dropped call means you're still blessed.
With every login, we unite,
In this jest, we find our light.

So if the signal dims or fades,
Dance with bytes, and join the parades.
Embrace the quirks, the fun, the thrill,
In every pixel, find your will.

Transmitting Moments of Clarity

In seconds flat, we share our day,
Through memes and gifs, we find our way.
Transmitting smiles, loading fun,
Life is wild when we just run.

Wi-Fi whispers secrets sweet,
In every buzz, our hearts compete.
Hold your phone, don't miss the chance,
To join the world in this dance.

Signal strong, humor bright,
Life's a joke that feels just right.
Glitches happen, breathe it in,
From every fall, we rise again.

So gather round, let laughter soar,
In wi-fi zones, we find our core.
Transmit your joy, connect the dots,
In life's funny game, we tie our knots.

Routing toward Revelation

In a world of bits and bytes,
Connection sparks the funny sights.
Lost in bandwidth, found in memes,
Life's a joke, or so it seems.

Ping me, please, I'm feeling low,
Buffering thoughts, where did they go?
Wi-Fi signals, dancing bright,
Laughing echoes, day and night.

Searching networks, seeking truth,
Router wisdom of our youth.
In the chaos, joy will reign,
Wi-Fi wonder, dull the pain.

Sipping data, sipping tea,
Streaming laughter, wild and free.
In the cloud, let's take a dive,
Funny circuits keep us alive.

Hacking Happiness

Crack the code of joy, my friend,
Signal strength that's hard to bend.
Laughter's upload, viral cheer,
Wi-Fi giggles, crystal clear.

Find a hotspot, make a call,
In this network, we won't fall.
Streaming smiles in every room,
Happiness, a wireless bloom.

Caffeine fixes, Wi-Fi grips,
Jokes and memes in tasty sips.
Hacker's glee in every byte,
Life's a pun, and it feels right.

Disconnect to reconnect,
In the chaos, we reflect.
Hacking hearts, it's worth the risk,
Life's a joke, so take a brisk.

Messages Between Moments

Every moment, data flows,
Texting truths, a laugh that glows.
In each ping, a tale entwines,
Life's a Wi-Fi, full of signs.

Stuck on loading, don't despair,
A funny meme waits in the air.
Connection drops, but not the cheer,
Messages bounce back, crystal clear.

Between the signals, laughter lies,
In the glitches, humor flies.
Through the chaos of the net,
Life's a chat we won't forget.

Check the stats, update the mind,
In the waiting, joy you'll find.
Every byte, a smile it sends,
In the network, fun transcends.

Discovering the Hidden Threads

Follow wires to find the truth,
Hidden threads from our first youth.
In the circuits, laughter hums,
Funny tales, where wisdom comes.

Texting life in every tone,
Wi-Fi waves and laughs we've known.
Lost the signal? Don't you fret,
Thread the needle, no regret.

Jokes uploaded in the night,
Finding joy, a pure delight.
Connecting hearts with every laugh,
Wi-Fi giggles, our autographed.

In the router, life's great jest,
Connect the dots, ignore the rest.
In the shadows, fun will bloom,
Hidden threads, a joyful room.

The Search for Signal Strength

In a world of bars that rise and fall,
We chase the signal, we heed the call.
Between the routers, we take our stance,
Hoping to join the great data dance.

We search for green lights, we scour the space,
As packets travel at a frantic pace.
Wi-Fi's our compass, our guide through night,
Connecting the dots in pixelated light.

With each lost signal, we sigh and fret,
Is it the phone, or is it the net?
But when we find that sweet, sweet link,
We toast our phones with a soda drink.

So here's to the quest for bandwidth's bliss,
The trials, the errors, we can't dismiss.
In this digital age where we all connect,
Signal strength's king, we must protect!

Spirals of Connection

In the web of waves, we're all entwined,
A spiral of connections, intertwined.
Lost in the ether, we laugh and grieve,
In our parentheses, we choose to believe.

Each blip, each bump, a reminder we're here,
In loading circles, we persevere.
Buffering dreams are just parts of the game,
Flinging our voices, who's to blame?

The ghosts of networks dance in our heads,
While memes and pings weave our threads.
We surf the spirals, both high and low,
For connection's a journey we all want to know.

So let's share our codes, our quirky delight,
In the stars of Wi-Fi, let's reunite.
Through signals unknown, may our laughter last,
In this whirl of data, we'll have a blast!

Bonded by Bandwidth

Here we are, folks, on this digital ride,
Bonded by bandwidth, we confide.
Streaming our lives in GIFs and snaps,
Uploading memories in perfect claptraps.

In the land of routers and fiber so fast,
Our friendships thrive, it's a wondrous cast.
With every connection, we feel the cheer,
Even with lag, we're drawing near.

When pixels blur and the screen goes shy,
We'll laugh it off, just you and I.
For in the jungle of a Wi-Fi dream,
Connection is realer than it may seem.

So let's toast to our buffering plight,
To the friendships formed in the endless byte.
With each little ping, our hearts will soar,
Bonded by bandwidth, forevermore!

The Art of Staying Connected

With a click and a tap, our world expands,
The art of staying in touch, it demands.
Through emojis and memes, we paint our days,
Connecting our lives in more funny ways.

Searching for outlets in cafes galore,
Yo, can I borrow your password? Oh, what a score!
In the land of Wi-Fi, we craft our art,
Every drop of data, a piece of our heart.

Through glitches and hiccups, we giggle away,
For every disconnection can't ruin our play.
Let's dance in the pixels, take flight on the screen,
In this digital world, we're all evergreen.

So here's to the routers that beam us alive,
To the chats that make us feel we can thrive.
In the art of connection, with laughter, let's flow,
Every Wi-Fi wave, a high-speed hello!

Routes to Unseen Realities

In a world of ones and zeroes,
We chase our signals high and low,
Searching for a drop of wisdom,
In bright screens that glow.

Sometimes we get disconnected,
Lost in a sea of buffering sighs,
Yet laughter bubbles through the chaos,
As memes and cats take to the skies.

Our routers guide our wildest dreams,
While updates promise vast delight,
Yet still we fumble through the cables,
In search of sheer wireless flight.

With every ping, a glimpse of truth,
In this digital comedy of lore,
We find that in the tangled web,
There's always room for more.

Pulsations of Presence

Connections pulse like disco lights,
In a dance of data waves so bright,
While our devices hum and buzz,
We ponder what this all does.

A signal drops, and we all scream,
As Wi-Fi turns into a dream,
We laugh as we command the void,
In messages that can't be destroyed.

We're surfing through the clouded skies,
Seeking truth with eager eyes,
Yet fluff and spam prevail the day,
While we giggle and scroll away.

So lift your phone and take a stance,
In this modern, pixelated dance,
For every blip and every beep,
Is life's reminder; it's not that deep.

The Space Between Packets

In the gap where whispers lie,
Between each data packet's flight,
We laugh at our connection woes,
As life updates on quirky flows.

A dropped call feels like a ghost,
Who plays hard to get, just for boast,
Yet in those lags and stillness found,
Laughter echoes all around.

In buffering moments, wisdom glows,
As we sync with all we chose,
Imagine this virtual delight,
As everything gets a playful bite.

So let's embrace this pixel pie,
Where humor's just a ping away,
In bytes of joy, the memes unite,
Finding magic in our digital plight.

Mapping the Wireless Soul

We wander through the W-Fi woods,
Collecting data like we should,
In every blink and every chime,
Our laughter transcends all time.

Each hotspot shines a beacon bright,
Leading us to strange, sweet sights,
With every lag and every freeze,
We find our pace, our heart's own breeze.

The stream of life flows fast and free,
A comedy of connectivity,
Yet in the silence, we can hear,
The joyous giggles drawing near.

As we navigate this wireless fate,
Embracing quirks with love innate,
We map our souls with every laugh,
In tech, we find our truest path.

Juggling Jargon

In a world of drops and boosts,
We chase the signal, quite the roost.
IP addresses dance and twirl,
While we just download dreams and whirl.

Requests fly high, like circus tricks,
A juggler's game with endless ticks.
The router's laughter fills the air,
As bytes and bits become our fare.

Connections made, then lost, oh dear,
A floating network of good cheer.
We find our fate in packets sent,
In every glitch and sweet content.

So here we stand, in Wi-Fi's glow,
With every meme, our spirits grow.
In this odd world, we tap and swipe,
Finding joy in every type.

The Unseen Web

Invisible threads connect us tight,
We surf through giggles every night.
Pixels and pings bring us together,
Laughing at life, no matter the weather.

We send a meme, it flies so fast,
A web of laughter that's built to last.
Lost in the clouds, we float on high,
With every update, we learn to try.

Anonymous friends in a pixelated space,
We share our quirks in cyberspace.
With every message, a wink or a grin,
In this unseen web, we learn to spin.

So grab your phone, don't let it sleep,
For digital love is ours to keep.
In the network's embrace, we dance and play,
Finding our path in the light of the day.

Data and Destiny

Data flows like a river wide,
In bits and bytes, we take our ride.
Binary tales, we twist and bend,
As ones and zeros become our friends.

In every login, a chance to laugh,
With every glitch, we find our path.
Our destiny mapped in a signal stream,
Living the dream, or so it seems.

Downloads, uploads, a life in flux,
Stumbling through life, oh what a luck!
We trade our quirks for bandwidth's grace,
Finding sweetness in every embrace.

So here we sit, as bytes collide,
Embracing the chaos, with tech as our guide.
In this digital dance, we take our flight,
Laughing our way into the night.

The Poetry of Protocol

In the realm of codes, rules are laid,
A protocol's dance, in laughter we wade.
With every packet, a verse we write,
Living the joy of the digital light.

A handshake here, a timeout there,
With every glitch, we learn to care.
Our stories unfold in the net's embrace,
Each connection made, a smiling face.

So we share our memes, and poke some fun,
In this world of data, we all can run.
Through routers and switches, we find delight,
Laughing together, buzzing like light.

And if the signal wavers, oh the jest,
For in this chaos, we're truly blessed.
With every refresh, life starts anew,
In the poetry of protocol, we find our view.

Eternal Uploads

In the cloud, my dreams take flight,
Packets zooming left and right.
Buffering is a test of fate,
Wi-Fi's love, oh, isn't it great?

Lost connections come and go,
But in my heart, the signal flows.
I swipe my fate with just a click,
Eternal uploads—what a trick!

I search for joy in every link,
But sometimes it just makes me think.
A 404 in matters of the heart,
Is this the way? Just play my part?

When the router hums a soothing sound,
I find my solace underground.
It's all a game, this pixel play,
So let's surf life—come what may!

Syncing with Serenity

In a world of endless streams,
I find my peace in data dreams.
Each bar on my device is hope,
Syncing with life's kaleidoscope.

Error messages make me frown,
Is it time to put my phone down?
But wait! There's joy in every press,
A giggle found in this data mess.

Connection drops? Just laugh it off,
Life's just a game of hide and scoff.
My smile's a signal strong and bright,
In this funny cosmic byte!

I ride the waves of bits and bytes,
Chasing dreams in router flights.
So here I stand, with gigabytes,
Finding joy in digital delights.

Life Beyond the Login

Log in, log out, what a ride,
In this vast digital tide.
I swipe with glee, I scroll with might,
Life's a meme, oh what a sight!

Password prompts, my daily test,
Sometimes I wonder what's best.
A funny face or cute cat pic,
Life's a joke—let's take a kick!

I share my thoughts in bytes so small,
And laugh at life through the firewall.
With friends online, we're never alone,
Together in this happy zone.

So raise your phone, let's take a shot,
In this crazy world, we'll connect a lot.
Beyond the login, life's a spree,
With every laugh, we'll sing with glee!

Networked Notions

In a web of thoughts, I weave and twist,
Finding humor in each little mist.
Signal drops, but laughter stays,
Navigating life's comical maze.

I share my heart on trending streams,
Weaving love with funny memes.
In this network, we all belong,
Join the dance, sing the song!

From pings and dings to buffering woes,
Life's full of jokes and silly prose.
Let's laugh together, share the mirth,
In our networked notions, there's great worth.

So here's to us, in the digital din,
With every hiccup, let the fun begin!
For in this realm of bits and bytes,
We find our joy in silly delights.

The Lighthouse of Life Lessons

In the signals we trust, like a lighthouse beam,
Lost in the waves of the internet's dream,
Buffering moments, we ride the slight lag,
Finding wise thoughts in a cat video tag.

Logins and passwords, a never-ending chore,
Updates pop up, who could ask for more?
Yet in this chaos, a lesson so clear,
Wi-Fi connects us—long-distance, my dear.

When the router's down, we all face despair,
A moment of quiet, an outage to share.
Laughter erupts when the pixels all freeze,
Life's like a signal; it's meant to tease.

So here's to the networks, the glitches, the quirks,
In this digital maze, let's embrace all the perks,
For life's little lessons, let's give a cheer,
Wi-Fi's our compass, our laughter's frontier!

Threading the Digital Needle

Connectivity's the thread; we weave it so tight,
In the fabric of friendship, we share the light.
Pixels and emojis, our needle's sweet grace,
In a world going viral, we find our place.

Wi-Fi's a needle, threading us close,
Binding our stories like a well-chosen prose.
Keep your signal strong, or it's bang, crash, crash!
Who knew deep talks could come from a flash?

When the Wi-Fi drops, all hope feels so slim,
But laughter erupts; our life's in the whim.
Scroll through our memories, some awkward, some cool,
In this online circus, we're all the same fool.

Patch up those devices, don't let them sit still,
Let's connect to the moments that give us a thrill.
For in digital chaos, joy's what we glean,
Life's just a meme, on this crazy machine!

Disconnect to Reconnect

Put down your devices, let's take a pause,
A virtual break, let's give it a cause.
With FOMO kicking in, we'll dance with delight,
In a world without Wi-Fi, we'll find the light.

Neighbors once strangers start sharing some glee,
Convos in person, as true as can be.
We unlock our hearts, without lag or delay,
No buffering moments, just a soulful display.

When the router resets, we'll gather and cheer,
Reconnecting with laughter, that's music to hear.
So pick up a book or a swing at the park,
Life's a bit better when we unplug the dark.

In tangible moments, friendships will thrive,
For the best connections keep the spirit alive.
With a wink and a smile, we're rolling the dice,
Life's richer, I swear, when we disconnect—nice!

Illuminating the Invisible

In the glow of the screen, insights arise,
Life lessons hidden behind thoughtful guise.
Wi-Fi waves dancing, they crack and they spin,
Unseen connections, where the fun begins.

Behind every password, a story untold,
Mysteries beckon, like digital gold.
With memes and GIFs, our laughter ignites,
In the vast cyber sea, we reach dizzying heights.

The router hums sweetly, a comforting drone,
In this pixelated realm, we're never alone.
But too much of this glow can make spirits dim,
So let's add some sunlight, go out on a whim.

For life's more than signals and bandwidth combined,
It's the humor we share, the joy intertwined.
So here's to uncovering what's witty and bright,
In the world of the unseen, let's revel tonight!

Ubiquitous Reverberations

In every corner, signals soar,
Connecting hearts like never before.
A blinking light, a dance on screens,
Life's true purpose in digital dreams.

We tap and swipe with glee each day,
Lost in memes that lead astray.
Yet through the bytes, we find our way,
A quirky path we gladly pay.

With every lag, our patience wears,
Yet still we scroll without a care.
Through ups and downs, we chase the ping,
In pixelated worlds, we are the kings.

So here's to life, a Wi-Fi spree,
Where buffering leads to mystery.
We search for joy in every byte,
And laugh together through the night.

Sacred Signals

In sacred waves, our spirits sing,
A strong connection is the thing.
With routers blessed and passwords true,
We find our purpose in memes anew.

The login page, a quest divine,
To unlock treasures you can't confine.
With every click, our joy expands,
In cyberspace, we take a stand.

Though outages may strike with force,
We forge ahead, we stay the course.
For in the chaos, laughter blooms,
As we chase signals through the rooms.

So let's embrace the quirky quests,
Where buffering is just a test.
In sacred signals, we unite,
And laugh at life into the night.

The Frequency of Fulfillment

In the frequency of our delight,
We surf the net both day and night.
With every ping, our hearts align,
In this vast web, we feel divine.

We giggle at the funny fails,
As memes and cats come through the trails.
In every swipe, a lesson rests,
The world is wild, but we are blessed.

With every signal that comes our way,
We find our fun in disarray.
From texts to snaps, our joy is surfed,
In this crazy net, we are well-versed.

So let's raise a toast to Wi-Fi bliss,
In tangled connections, we find our kiss.
With laughter as our constant guide,
We ride the waves of life with pride.

Resonance Within the Router

Inside the router, magic brews,
With every wave, new laughter ensues.
Connections spark like matches bright,
In digital realms, everything feels right.

Through glitches small, we persevere,
With funny memes, we share good cheer.
In microseconds, friendships grow,
A networked life, a brilliant show.

As signals fade, we hold our ground,
In buffering spaces, joy is found.
We laugh aloud at every drop,
And start again, we never stop.

So here's to life, a Wi-Fi ride,
With jokes and smiles, we're full of pride.
In every connection, humor reigns,
And echoes through our Wi-Fi veins.

Heartbeats and Hotspots

In a world where signals fly,
We chase the bars that lift us high.
Connection glitches, laughter spills,
We find our joy in Wi-Fi thrills.

Life's a dance of pings and tones,
With buffering dreams and pixelated phones.
We surf the waves of fleeting bliss,
A hotspot hug, we can't resist!

Echoes of Connectivity

In coffee shops, we sit and scroll,
While Wi-Fi waves take center role.
Chatting with friends, a meme or two,
Life's a screen and we're all in queue.

Glitches happen, we burst with glee,
Life's a router—can you see?
Giggle fits at failed uploads,
Who knew wisdom's in these codes?

Code of the Cosmos

In zeros, ones, our truths align,
Streaming thoughts, like endless wine.
We scroll through life on digital lanes,
Wi-Fi signals, our silly chains.

Data dreams are what we chase,
In cosmic clouds, we find our space.
With every drop, a jest reborn,
Life's a buffer, just hold on!

Virtual Verses

In cyberspace, we write our tales,
With links and likes, the humor sails.
A tweet of wisdom here and there,
In virtual verses, life laid bare.

Each upload brings a joyful cheer,
Memes and laughter redefining fear.
In this funny web we weave,
Both signal lost and hearts believe.

Signals in the Ether

In the air, a dance of beams,
We chase the Wi-Fi like dreams.
To connect is our silly game,
But dropped calls sure bring us shame.

With routers playing hide and seek,
A signal strong, we shout and squeak.
In search of bars like some lost souls,
We trip on wires, oh, how it rolls!

We sit and scroll, lost in our screens,
Laughing hard at memes and scenes.
Yet all we crave in bytes and bites,
Is just a signal that ignites!

So raise your device, toast the router,
Let's stream our joy; let fun sprout her.
In this digital age, we thrive,
With every signal, we're alive!

Connection's Paradox

I turn it off, then back on too,
In hopes my apps will dare pursue.
Yet every pause feels like a plight,
Connection lost, what a funny sight!

A friend texts me, his screen just froze,
While my own signal oddly glows.
Did I jinx it with my jest?
Let's laugh instead, it's for the best!

Though bandwidth shrinks like my free time,
I find the humor in the rhyme.
We stumble through this digital maze,
Where every hiccup sparks our gaze.

So let's be silly, let's embrace,
The whims of Wi-Fi in this race.
For in each glitch, there's joy to find,
In our connections, humor's entwined!

Bandwidth Beyond Boundaries

We quest for speed, we seek that flow,
But often face a buffer's woe.
Yet hidden in these pixel fights,
Are stories worth a thousand bytes.

When signals drop, we start to bicker,
But humor's champ, it makes us snicker.
In every freeze, we see the fun,
Life's Wi-Fi game has just begun!

Behind this screen, we find our tribe,
Connected hearts, our joy's vibe.
So let's embrace this crazy ride,
For laughter's the best Wi-Fi guide!

In the end, it's not about speed,
But joy we share, that's all we need.
Let's laugh through lag, and cheer the ping,
In this wild world, let our hearts sing!

The Pulse of Digital Existence

In a world of networks, we reside,
With emojis flying far and wide.
Our lives a stream, a playful chase,
A quirky dance in this cyberspace.

With every login, a choice we make,
A fun connection, or a wild break.
Yet in this chaos, we find our fun,
Sharing giggles until we're done.

So here's to memes that make us grin,
To every mouse click that's our win.
For in this digital life's delight,
We find the laughter that feels just right!

In bandwidth's surge, a pulse so real,
Let's cherish moments, that's the deal.
With every click, we feel alive,
In this playful dance, we thrive!

www.ingramcontent.com/pod-product-compliance
Lightning Source LLC
Chambersburg PA
CBHW051700160426
43209CB00004B/972